BORN

PARVATI KAAL

Precautions

Read if You Can

Who Is Parvati Kaal
A Fictional Character
Who Is Complete in Self
Parvati Is Energy
Kaal Is End or Time
Energy and Time
Completes Itself
Shiv the Atom
Or the One Who Is the Father
of Even Those Who Have
No Parents [Anath]
The One Who Has no One
Has Shiv Besides
The Father of Everyone and
Everything

Shiv Means the Endless End
The Entire Creation
Understand It in a Language ,
Art Form or in Whatever You
Are Good at or in Whatever
Way You Can
If You Are Too Good at
Something
It Probable You Become the
God of That Thing
Meaning You Become Perfect
And Perfection Exists in the
Perfect Itself
Trust
Have Faith
God's Watching
Everyone Has God
In Themselves
You Are One With God

And When You Realise That
It Is Only Then
You Don't Want Anything
In Life

You Are Complete
By Yourself
By the God Particle in You
By the Truth in You
And That Is the Ultimate

The Ultimate
Is You
The God Which Resides
In You
In Everyone
In Every Being
In Everything
Living or Non Living

Special Thanks To Shiv

What You Can Listen to
[Suggestions]
To Realise
What You Really Are
How Wrong You Were
How Stupid You Were
How Not You
You Were

Kaal Bhairav Ashtakam
Rudrashtakam
Gayatri Mantra
Lalitha Sahasranama

Music Is Not the Only Path To
Enlightenment

You Can Play Your Own
Created God's Music
Or Whatever
Or Even the Thing
Or Art or Whatever You Are
Good at
It Will Ultimately Lead You to
the Reset Rest
To the Ultimate
The Reality Inside You

When You Give Up on
Yourself
Always Remember
God Never Gives Up on You
Its Still There
Watching
And Waiting for You
To Be Perfect in Something

In Anything
Or Whatever You Like
Not To Die
But To Realise
For You May Call God by
Names
But It When You Remove Your
Own Name
Your Own Identity to
Nothingness
You Find the Truth Hidden
Inside You
The Real Truth
Which Is Far Beyond any
Conspiracy
Or any Reality We Live in
And That Is
We all Are Made Up of the
Same Matter

Or the Same Construct
We Are One
In the End
Believe It or Not
You Are Neither Different
Nor Special
Not Anything or Anyone
You Believe
You Are Not Even You
But Just a Mere Part of This
Maya
Of This Created World
Part of the Endless End
A Part Which Can Never
Apart Itself

No Matter What
I Reside in You
You in Me

God in Us
In Everyone
Even in the Atheists

Even in the Non Living

Everyone
Everything Is the Same
Its Not Manifest
But Understanding
The Not
The Not of Nothingness
The Empty
The Whatever You Call It
Its Just There

You Understand When You Do
There Is no Other Ways to It

End Is Permanent
You Will Die
One Day
But for That Day
Is Today or Maybe Not
It Is Not in Your Hands
Give It Up To God
In Whichever God You Believe

Leave It Up to Time

Don't Care

Don't Bother

Life Is Endless

It Is Beyond
The Human Perception

And One More Thing
Probably
You Should Never Mess Up
Or Introduce God
In Your Life
If You Don't Want To Get Out
of the Daily Loop You Are in

Don't Look Up
Look Inside Yourself

There Resides
A Part of God in You

Be Careful Not To Awake It
It Not Only Brings You Near
To Your Death or Not
Who Knows ?

I Am Not God Neither Good
I Am Not a Human
I Am Not
I Am Not Even the Not
But Still There Is Something
Something I Don't Know
And I Accept
That I Don't Know
I Apologise to my Future Self
Which Resides Somewhere
in the Eternity
For I Don't Really Understand
What I Did With my Life

But for Whatever It Was

It Was Worth Knowing
One Thing

It's Not About Human
Or the God or the Source
But the Weirdness
Which Resided in Me
It Was Realised Only
In the Name of God

So I Won't Take Anything
With Me When I Die
We Don't Take Anything
Nothing
We Reside in Nothingness
And This Nothingness Is
Eternal

For There Is Nothing More
Pure
Than Nothingness Itself

For Whatever Happens Next
Is Predestined
It Is Already Written

Maybe It Is Not for
Me To Know

Or To Understand

But Always Remember

You Are Nothing

And You Will Always Remain
Nothing , no Matter What
Or Where You Are Today
But
In the End

The End
Is Eventually the Same
No Matter How Long You Live
You Live or You Don't
But It Still Will Be the Same
For Everyone and Everything

Next page

On how you were born

And how you should live

For example

I was born
Left alone
No one loved me
Or I believed to believe so
I craved for love
For belongings
For everything
But then
Nothing changed
Until god introduced itself
into my life

Its happens
I still don't understand it fully
Not that capable perhaps
Still egoistic and stupid
But for whatever it is
God really gave me the way
in the end

what happens when you are
born ?

you are born into the world
of unknown
thinking this is my family ,
my fate , my pears ,
my friends
but what if its true and not at
the same time ?

what if what you think of it to
be is real and not at the
same time

don't quite reading

when did it all start

even i am unaware
and unsure

but for whatever i could
understand

is that this is a long game

being played since forever
and ever

why though ? who did it ?
why is this all happening ?

i don't know

but someone does
Maybe I don't know

things you have to do in and
not be a mere weirdo which i
became just to realise
How bad I was

you have to do multiple
things in one time

music
¬!"£$%^&*()_+
¬ " £
#~~~#~}@@

~!@#$%^&*()
!)

~!@#$%^&*(!)

learn to focus

Peripheral vision is the ability
to see things where you are
not directly looking
"out of the corner
of your eye."

Even in young people with
normal vision,
peripheral vision is poor

Feeling challenged or
provoked

That is good

Because you can only find
when you don't want to
I still really don't want to
Or maybe I do

Or maybe I don't know

My thoughts keep changing

Swinging

Drastically

Highly vulnerable
to what I see , read and even
made to think

What about you

Who's reading

Anyone ?
Stupid things
playing stupid games

One day every will suffer
you idiots , who is this I ask ?
Me and my ego
Can't blame your parents
When you have been the
noob all along
You couldn't see
Because you didn't want to
They were trying to tell you
all along
Since the beginning
That something is wrong
But it was you
who couldn't understand
It was you All along
You couldn't bear
to see
a thing change
Even when it was changing

When everything was
progressing to change
already

You couldn't bear to see the
difference
Even when you felt that
something isn't right

It was always near you
In you
But still it wasn't you

You were playful
Joyful
Were dreaming and reading
fairy tales
In hopes of a better world

Which never existed in the
first place
You couldn't bother to
tolerate the real you who you
would be after knowing what
you shouldn't be

In the midst of chaos you will
find yourself out
In the midst of your own
temper
You will pave your new way
to the round about
Which is not in the round
about by the way
Its inside you

They were always provoking
your thoughts

But you just couldn't see
Beyond yourself
You even wrote the things
Which were thrown at you
But still could never
understand it
Until one day when you did
You released
Its still nothing
Everything still remains in
nothing . for this nothing will
last forever and now that I
write this I do understand a
little bit perhaps but still I
accept that I don't know
And I wish for everyone who
doesn't don't face the same
end as me but they better

discover the real god which
resides in themselves
The universe which doesn't
resides in you
But how you are just
a mere part of it
Just the smallest
Just the nothing
The not of the nothing
Not even the not
But you are
Just as it is
Because you are
That's it
You are not you
Always remember not to
forget yourself because if
god reaches you anyhow
its more challenging to bear

www.ingramcontent.com/pod-product-compliance
Lightning Source LLC
La Vergne TN
LVHW020544160826
845677LV00015B/4198

* 9 7 9 8 3 7 4 9 2 9 3 8 6 *